First World War
and Army of Occupation
War Diary
France, Belgium and Germany

52 DIVISION
Divisional Troops
412 Field Company Royal Engineers
1 April 1918 - 31 May 1919

WO95/2893/2

The Naval & Military Press Ltd
www.nmarchive.com
Published in association with The National Archives

Published by

The Naval & Military Press Ltd

Unit 10 Ridgewood Industrial Park,

Uckfield, East Sussex,

TN22 5QE England

Tel: +44 (0) 1825 749494

www.naval-military-press.com

www.nmarchive.com

This diary has been reprinted in facsimile from the original. Any imperfections are inevitably reproduced and the quality may fall short of modern type and cartographic standards.

© **Crown Copyright**
Images reproduced by permission of The National Archives, London, England, 2015.

Contents

Document type	Place/Title	Date From	Date To
Heading	WO95/2893-2		
Heading	52nd Division 412th (Lowland) Fld Coy R.E. Apr 1918-Apr 1919		
Heading	52nd Divisional Engineers Disembarked Marseilles From Egypt 17.4.18. 412th (Lowland) Field Company R.E April 1918		
Heading	War Diary Of 412th (Low) Field Coy R.E From 1st April 1918 To 30th April 1918 Vol III No.10		
War Diary	Surafend (J18a.5.8 Palestine Sheet XIII)	01/04/1918	01/04/1918
War Diary	Kantara	02/04/1918	02/04/1918
War Diary	Alexandria	03/04/1918	03/04/1918
War Diary	Alexandria (Sidi Bishr)	04/04/1918	11/04/1918
War Diary	At Sea	12/04/1918	16/04/1918
War Diary	Marseilles	17/04/1918	19/04/1918
War Diary	On Rail	20/04/1918	21/04/1918
War Diary	Noyelles	22/04/1918	22/04/1918
War Diary	Arry	23/04/1918	29/04/1918
War Diary	Aire	30/04/1918	30/04/1918
Miscellaneous	Monthly Strength Statistics	31/03/1918	31/03/1918
Heading	War Diary Of 412th (Land) Field Coy R.E. From 1/4/18 To 30/4/18 Vol III No. 10		
Heading	War Diary Of 412th (Lowland) Fields Co R.E. from 1st May 1918 To 31st May 1918 Volume 3 No.11		
War Diary	Cohem (France Sheet 36a) H 2 b.	01/05/1918	01/05/1918
War Diary	Foret De Nieppe	02/05/1918	06/05/1918
War Diary	Aire	07/05/1918	07/05/1918
War Diary	Divion Aire	08/05/1918	08/05/1918
War Diary	Latargette (A 1 Central)	09/05/1918	31/05/1918
Miscellaneous	Monthly Strength Statistics		
Heading	War Diary Of 412th (Lowland) Field Coy RE From 1st May 1918 To 31st May 1918 Volume 3 No.11 (Month Of May 1918)		
Heading	War Diary Of 412th Low Field Coy R.E. From 1st June 1918 To 30th June 1918 Vol 3 No12		
Heading	War Diary Of 412th Lowland Field Coy R.E. Vol 3 No.12 From 1.6.18 To 30.6.18		
War Diary	La Targette A1 Central	01/06/1918	30/06/1918
Miscellaneous	Monthly Strength Statistics		
Heading	War Diary Of 412th Lowland Field Coy R.E From 30.6.18 To 31.7.18 Volume 3 No13		
Heading	War Diary Of 412th Lowland Field Coy R.E From 30.6.18 To 31.7.18 Volume 3 No. 13		
War Diary	La Targette A 1 Central	01/07/1918	22/07/1918
War Diary	Barlin Q.2.b.4.6	23/07/1918	30/07/1918
War Diary	Ecoivres	31/07/1918	31/07/1918
Miscellaneous	Monthly Strength Statistics		
Heading	War Diary Of 412th (Low) Field Coy R.E. From 1/8/18 To 31/8/18 Vol. 4 No. 2		
Heading	War Diary Of 412th (Lowland) Field Coy R.E From 31/8/18 To 31/8/18 Vol 4 No.2		

War Diary	Ecurie A 28 C	01/08/1918	16/08/1918
War Diary	La Maison Rouge D12c	17/08/1918	20/08/1918
War Diary	Lattre St Quentin J.24.c	21/08/1918	22/08/1918
War Diary	Bretencourt R 27 C. 8.9	23/08/1918	24/08/1918
War Diary	Mercatel Switch S.3.a.0.5.	25/08/1918	26/08/1918
War Diary	S.5.b.4.8.	24/08/1918	31/08/1918
Miscellaneous	Monthly Strength Statistics	31/07/1918	31/07/1918
Heading	War Diary Of 412th Lowland Field Coy R.E From 1-9-18 To 30-9-18 Vol 4 No.3		
War Diary	Croisilles T 23a 85	01/09/1918	03/09/1918
War Diary	Queant D2 Central	04/09/1918	08/09/1918
War Diary	St Ledger T.27.a.3.6	09/09/1918	16/09/1918
War Diary	Queant D.2 Central	17/09/1918	30/09/1918
Miscellaneous	Monthly Strength Statistics	31/08/1918	31/08/1918
Heading	War Diary Of 412th Lowland Field Coy R.E From 1.9.18 To 30.9.18 Vol 4 No.3		
Heading	War Diary Of 412th Lowland Field Coy R.E Vol 4 No 3 Month Of October 1918		
Heading	War Diary Of 412th Lowland Field Coy R.E Vol 4 No 3 Month Of October		
War Diary	Moeuvres E.20.a.5	01/10/1918	01/10/1918
War Diary	Graincourt (K6.a.2.4)	02/10/1918	02/10/1918
War Diary	Graincourt K6a 24	03/10/1918	06/10/1918
War Diary	Beaumetz (J7 Central)	07/10/1918	07/10/1918
War Diary	Villers Sir Simon (I 5a 8.8)	08/10/1918	09/10/1918
War Diary	Denier I 19.c.6.9	10/10/1918	19/10/1918
War Diary	Chateau De La Haie	20/10/1918	20/10/1918
War Diary	Billy Montigny (O.26.d)	21/10/1918	21/10/1918
War Diary	Auby (q 33 A 61)	22/10/1918	23/10/1918
War Diary	Rache R32c24	24/10/1918	25/10/1918
War Diary	Orchies G23a76	26/10/1918	27/10/1918
War Diary	Le Saubois	28/10/1918	31/10/1918
Miscellaneous	Monthly Strength Statistics	30/09/1916	30/09/1916
Heading	War Diary Of 412th (Lowland) Field Coy R.E. Vol No. 4 No.4		
War Diary	Le Saubois O6c.3.7	01/11/1918	11/11/1918
War Diary	Hergnies G.1.3.7.	12/11/1918	12/11/1918
War Diary	Sirault J.6.4.2	13/11/1918	19/11/1918
War Diary	Ghlin Kl.85.45	20/11/1918	25/11/1918
War Diary	Masnuy St Pierre	26/11/1918	26/11/1918
War Diary	E.14.b.3.7	30/11/1918	30/11/1918
Miscellaneous	Monthly Strength Statistics	31/10/1918	31/10/1918
Heading	War Diary Of 412th (Lowland) Field Coy RE From 1/11/18 To 30/11/18 Month Of November 1918 Vol 4 No.4		
Heading	War Diary Of 412th (Lowland) Field Coy RE From 1st December 1918 To 31st December 1918 (Volume 4 No 6)		
War Diary	Masnuy St Pierre E.14.b.3.7	01/12/1918	13/12/1918
War Diary	Louvignies W1bb 8.8	14/12/1918	31/12/1918
Miscellaneous	Monthly Strength Statistics	30/11/1918	30/11/1918
Heading	War Diary Of 412th (Lowland) Field Coy R.E. From 1st December 1918 To 31st December 1918		
Heading	War Diary 412 (Lowland) Field Coy. R.E. Month Of January 1919 Vol. 4. No. 8.		
War Diary	Louvignies W1bb 8.8	01/01/1919	01/01/1919

Type	Description	From	To
War Diary	Belgium Sheet : 38 1:40.000 Edition 2	02/01/1919	31/01/1919
Miscellaneous	Monthly Strength Statistics	31/12/1918	31/12/1918
Heading	War Diary Of 412th (Lowland) Field Company Royal Engineers 1st February To 28th February 1919		
War Diary	Louvignies	01/02/1919	28/02/1919
War Diary	Monthly Strength Statistics		
Miscellaneous	Strength Statistic (Actual)	01/03/1919	01/03/1919
Heading	War Diary For Month March 1919		
War Diary	Louvignies Hainaut Belgium	01/03/1919	23/03/1919
War Diary	Soignies Hainaut Belgium	24/03/1919	31/03/1919
Miscellaneous	Monthly Strength Statistics	31/03/1919	31/03/1919
Heading	War Diary 412th Lowland Field Co Royal Engineers.		
War Diary	Soignies	01/04/1919	03/04/1919
War Diary	Haucourt	04/04/1919	05/04/1919
War Diary	Belgium	06/04/1919	29/04/1919
Miscellaneous	Monthly Strength Statistic	01/05/1919	01/05/1919
Heading	War Diary 412 Fd Co R.E Month Of April 1919 Vol 5 No.4		
Heading	Diary Of 412th Lowland Field Coy Royal Engineers.		
War Diary	Soignies Belgium	01/05/1919	31/05/1919
Miscellaneous	Monthly Strength Statistic	01/06/1919	01/06/1919

noon 1/26/93 (2)

noon 1/28/93 (2)

52ND DIVISION

412TH(LOWLAND) FLD COY R.E.

APR 1918-APR 1919

52nd Divisional Engineers

Disembarked MARSEILLES from EGYPT 17.4.18.

412th (Lowland) FIELD COMPANY R. E.

APRIL 1918.

Vol 1

-: CONFIDENTIAL :-

WAR DIARY

OF

#12TH (LOWLAND) COY R.E.

FROM 1st APRIL 1918 TO 30th APRIL 1918.

VOL III   N° 10

Army Form C. 2118.

WAR DIARY
or
INTELLIGENCE SUMMARY.

(Erase heading not required.)

VOLUME 3. N° 10.

Instructions regarding War Diaries and Intelligence Summaries are contained in F. S. Regs., Part II. and the Staff Manual respectively. Title pages will be prepared in manuscript.

Place	Date	Hour	Summary of Events and Information	Remarks and references to Appendices
SURAFEND. (J189.5.8 Palestine Sheet XIII)	1-4-18	0700	Company proceeded to LUDD, entrained & left at 1330.	
KANTARA	2.4.18	0600	Arrive KANTARA. Entrained for ALEXANDRIA at 2200.	
ALEXANDRIA	3.4.18		Arrive ALEXANDRIA at 1000 & proceeded to TRANSIT CAMP SIDI BISHR.	
ALEXANDRIA (SIDI BISHR)	4.4.18		Awaiting embarkation orders	
"	5.4.18		" " " "	
"	6.4.18		" " " "	
"	7.4.18		" " " "	
"	8.4.18		" " " "	
"	9.4.18		" " " "	
"	10.4.18		Embarked on H.M.T. "OMRAH" at 1200. Sailed at 1400.	
AT SEA	11.4.18			
"	12.4.18			
"	13.4.18			
"	14.4.18			
"	15.4.18			
"	16.4.18			
MARSEILLES	17.4.18		Disembarked at 1400 & proceeded to "MUSSO'S REST CAMP	
"	18.4.18		"Musso's" Rest Camp	
ON RAIL	19.4.18		Entrained at 0900.	
"	20.4.18			
"	21.4.18			
NOYELLES	22.4.18		Detrained at NOYELLES at 0800 and proceeded to ARRY (SOMME)	
ARRY	23.4.18		Company engaged in intensive training. (Musketry, Bayonet fighting & Gas Drill) Re-equipping	
"	24.4.18		Company engaged as on 23.4.18	
"	25.4.18		" " " "	
"	26.4.18		" " " "	
"	27.4.18		" " " "	
"	28.4.18		" " " "	
"	29.4.18		Proceeded to RUE and entrained.	
AIRE	30.4.18		Detrained at AIRE at 0430 and proceeded to COHEM. (FRANCE. SHEET 36A. H.2.b.)	

Army Form C. 2118.

WAR DIARY
or
INTELLIGENCE SUMMARY.
(Erase heading not required.)

Instructions regarding War Diaries and Intelligence Summaries are contained in F. S. Regs., Part II. and the Staff Manual respectively. Title pages will be prepared in manuscript.

Place	Date	Hour	Summary of Events and Information	Remarks and references to Appendices
	3/3/18		Monthly Strength Statistics	

	Effective Strength	Ration Strength	Detached for Duty	Admitted to Field Ambulance / Stretcher Strength
Casualties during Month	O. 860 / 4. 209	O. 860 / 6. 40	O. 0 / 1. 59	O. 860 / 1. -
Strength of Strength:- Officers Other Ranks	- 3 / 1 / 6. 206			
Taken on Strength O. 861 Other Ranks	4. 1			
	6. 213	6. 204	-	6. -

A.F.C. 2118

Confidential
War Diary
of
14th (od) West Co RE

From 1/4/18
To 30/4/18

Vol III No 10

Vol 1

Month of May 1918.

Vol 2

Confidential.

War Diary
of
412th (Lowland) Field Co. R.E.
from 1st May 1918
to 31st May 1918

Volume 3.   No 11.

Army Form C. 2118.

WAR DIARY
or
INTELLIGENCE SUMMARY.
(Erase heading not required.)

Month of May 1918.

VOLUME 3   N° 11.

Instructions regarding War Diaries and Intelligence Summaries are contained in F.S. Regs., Part II. and the Staff Manual respectively. Title pages will be prepared in manuscript.

Place	Date	Hour	Summary of Events and Information	Remarks and references to Appendices
COHEM (FRANCE SHEET 5A) H2b 36a FORET DE NIEPPE	1/5/18	0900	Coy moves to (5F.8.16) (France-Sheet 5A) Coy came under orders of C.R.E. 5th Divn.	
	2-5-18		Coy engages on MORBECQUE – HAVERSKERQUE Defence Line. One section proceeds to Coo.	
	3-5-18		Coy engages as on 2/5/18. Reserve Line 3 sentry posts built and one partly excavated. 3000 yards communication jumper trench. Strap deep excavated.	
	4-5-18		" " "	
	5-5-18		" " "	
AIRE	6-5-18	0900	Coy rejoins 52nd Army at AIRE (5.E.75.90) (France-Sheet 5A)	
	7-5-18		Futurepost Section moves to DIVION (1G.05.65) (France-Sheet Lens)	
DIVION	8-5-18	1800	" " " LATARGETTE (H1 Central – France Sheet 7 ARDEVIL)	
AIRE			Coy entrains at AIRE.	
LATARGETTE (H1 central)	9-5-18	0500	Coy arrives at LA TARGETTE.	
	10-5-18		Overhauling Battery Plants at NEUVILLE ST VAAST (A9a) & BERTHONVAL FARM. (F4d). Overhauling Plant at D.H.Q. Repairing & improving BROWN LINE. Maintenance of Land Mines. Lewis Gun training.	
	11-5-18		Coy engages as on 10-5-18.	
	12-5-18		" " "	
	13-5-18		" " " 12-5-18. Repairing & improving Wagon Roads for Artillery. Wire's so trestial	
	14-5-18		Overhauling Bathing Plant at NEUVILLE ST VAAST & BERTHONVAL FARM. Overhauling & repairing Plant at D.H.Q. Repairing & improving BROWN LINE. Maintenance of Land Mines. Taking down & erecting Stables at D.H.Q. Lewis Gun training.	
	15-5-18		Coy. engages as on 14-5-18. & Overhauling Electric Plant for Byles in the Line.	
	16-5-18		Coy engages as on 15-5-18. R.E works in Right Sub-section of Divnl. Line taken over & Back loading Signal Station, Air Foots etc repaired	
	17-5-18		Coy engages as on 16-5-18 FARBUS Post at B.7. A.S.S. Wires with Single Appearance

Army Form C. 2118.

WAR DIARY
or
INTELLIGENCE SUMMARY.
(Erase heading not required.)

Instructions regarding War Diaries and Intelligence Summaries are contained in F.S. Regs., Part II. and the Staff Manual respectively. Title pages will be prepared in manuscript.

Place	Date	Hour	Summary of Events and Information	Remarks and references to Appendices
LA TARGETTE (A1 central)	18-5-18		Maintenance of Electric lighting Plant at H.Q. of Bde in the Line. Overhaul of Pumps at D.H.Q. Taking down the existing Stables at D.H.Q. Excavation widening of FARBUS POST. Acrylic apron fences at SPUR POST. Subway under FARBUS ROAD. Survey of Right Sector Front Line. R.E. Work in Line; Gasproofing Dugouts. Laying, repairing, Duckboards. Repairing camouflage Screens.	
"	19-5-18		Coy. engaged as on 18-5-18.	
"	20-5-18		" " " 19-5-18, & installing 4. 200 gall Water Tanks at FARBUS	
"	21-5-18		" " " 20-5-18 & installing Dugouts (2) at FARBUS POST, & S at Battn. H.Q. THELUS CAVES	
"	22-5-18		Coy engages as on 21-5-18.	
"	23-5-18		" " " "	
"	24-5-18		" " " "	
"	25-5-18		Maintenance of Electric lighting Plant at H.Q. of Bde in the Line. Survey of Right Sector Front Line. R.E. works in Right Sector Front Line :- Laying, repairing Duckboards. Training & Repairing Revetted, Gasproofing M.G. Btn H.Q. Building Barricades. Repairing Dugouts. Repairing 2 NCOs with M.G. Battn. to Camouflage School, Medical Aid Posts Renders Shrapnel proof. Preparing M.G. Positions.	
"	26-5-18		Coy engaged as on 25-5-18	Emplacement dug & 4-200 gall Tanks installed at FARBUS.
"	27-5-18		" " " "	" 4-700 " " MORRISON DUMP.
"	28-5-18		" " " "	" 3-200 " " in POST LINE near WILLERVAL.
"	29-5-18		" " " "	
"	30-5-18		" " " "	2 Lewis Gun Teams trained
"	31-5-18		" " " "	

Army Form C. 2118.

WAR DIARY
or
INTELLIGENCE SUMMARY.
(Erase heading not required.)

Place	Date	Hour	Summary of Events and Information	Remarks and references to Appendices
			MONTHLY STRENGTH STATISTICS	
	30/4/18		CASUALTIES — DURING MONTH: O. ORs. — 10	
			STRENGTH:	
				Effective Strength	Ration Strength	Detached for Duty	Admitted to Field Amb Still on Strength
				O / ORs	O / ORs	O / ORs	O / ORs
				6 / 213	6 / 201	0 / 39	0 / 6
			STRENGTH: To Hospital — 10				
					203		
			TAKEN ON STRENGTH O / OR				
			Reinforcements from Base — 2 / 5				
			" U.K — 4				
	31/5/18			6 / 210	6 / 149	0 / 38	0 / 6

Month of May '18

Confidential
War Diary
of
412th (Lowlands) Field
Coy RE

From 1st May 1918
to 31st May 1918

Volume 3 N° 11.
(Month of MAY. 1918)

N 3

CONFIDENTIAL

War Diary
of
119th Field Coy Aust RE

From 1st June 1918
to 30th June 1918

Vol 3 No 12

CONFIDENTIAL

WAR DIARY OF

A 12th (LOWLAND) FIELD COY. R.E.

VOL. 3. N° 12.

From 1.6.18 TO. 30.6.18.

WAR DIARY or INTELLIGENCE SUMMARY

Army Form C. 2118.

MONTH OF JUNE   VOLUME 3   N° 12

(Erase heading not required.)

Place	Date	Hour	Summary of Events and Information	Remarks and references to Appendices
LA TARGETTE A1 CENTRAL	1-6-18		Maintenance of Electric Lighting Plant at HQRS of the Brigade on the line. Survey of Reg'tl sectors of Divisional Line. R.E. work in Reg'tl sectors of Divisional Line :- Laying & Repairing Duckboards, Draining & Repairing Trenches, Repairing & Re-profiling Dugouts. Clearing Camouflage Screens. Maintenance of Water Dumps at FARBUS, MORRISON & WILLERVAL. Installation of Water Dump at LONGWOOD. Construction of 2 Lotus Kilns. 2 N.C.Os with Machine Gun Batt'n preparing M.G. positions. 2 Lewis Gun teams trained. Maintenance of Agricultural Plot	
"	2-6-18			
"	3-6-18			
"	4-6-18			
"	5-6-18			
"	6-6-18			
"	7-6-18			
"	8-6-18		Maintenance of Electric Lighting Plant HQRS of the Brigade in the line. Survey of Reg'tl sectors of Divisional Line. R.E. work in Reg'tl sectors of Divisional Line:- Laying & Repairing Duckboards, Draining & Repairing Trenches, Repairing & Re-profiling Dugouts. Repairing Camouflage Screens. Maintenance of Water Dumps at FARBUS, MORRISON & WILLERVAL. Installation of Water Dump at LONGWOOD. (3-200 gallon tanks). Installation of Small English Meters. 2 N.C.Os with M.G. Batt'n preparing M.G. positions. Maintenance of Agricultural Plot.	
"	9-6-18			
"	10-6-18			
"	11-6-18			
"	12-6-18			
"	13-6-18			
"	14-6-18			
"	15-6-18 to 21-6-18		NIL	
"	22-6-18		Maintenance of Electric Lighting Plant at HQRS of the Brigade on the line. Survey of Reg'tl sectors of Divisional Line. R.E. work in Reg'tl sectors of Divisional Line :- Laying & Repairing Duckboards, Draining & Repairing Trenches, Repairing & Re-profiling Dugouts. Repairing Camouflage Screens. Maintenance of Water Dumps at FARBUS, MORRISON & WILLERVAL. Installation of Water Dump at LONGWOOD. (3-200 gallon tanks) Installation of Small English Shelters. 2 N.C.Os with M.G. Batt'n preparing M.G. positions. Repairing Trench pumps. Renewing wire line. Maintenance of Agricultural Plot.	
"	23-6-18			
"	24-6-18			
"	25-6-18			
"	26-6-18			
"	27-6-18			
"	28-6-18			
"	29-6-18			
"	30-6-18			

Army Form C. 2118.

WAR DIARY
or
INTELLIGENCE SUMMARY.

(Erase heading not required.)

Instructions regarding War Diaries and Intelligence Summaries are contained in F. S. Regs., Part II. and the Staff Manual respectively. Title pages will be prepared in manuscript.

Place	Date	Hour	Summary of Events and Information					Remarks and references to Appendices
			MONTHLY STRENGTH STATISTICS					
				Effective Strength	Ration Strength	Detached for Duty	Admitted to Field Amb Sick on Strength	
					O	ORs		O	ORs		O	ORs		O	ORs	
	31·5·18		CASUALTIES DURING MONTH	0	0	0	0	0	0	0	0	
			STRUCK OFF STRENGTH:	6	210	6	149	0	38	0	6	
			To Hospital - Sick O ORs 9									
			" " Wounded 4									
			" " Killed 3									
				-	16							
				6	194							
			TAKEN ON STRENGTH:-									
			Reinforcements from Base O. ORs 1. 4									
			" " Hospital - 1									
			" " U.K. - 3									
				1	11							
	30·6·18			4	205	5	149	1	26	1	·	

CONFIDENTIAL

WAR DIARY
OF
#1/2ND (LOWLAND) FIELD COY. R.E.

FROM 30.6.14
TO 31.4.18

VOLUME 3   No 13

VR 4

War Diary of
A.127th London (Field) Coy. R.E.
From 30-6-18 to 31-4-18
Volume 3 No. 13

Confidential

Army Form C. 2118.

WAR DIARY or INTELLIGENCE SUMMARY.
(Erase heading not required.)

Month of July 1918
VOLUME 4. No. 1

Place	Date	Hour	Summary of Events and Information	Remarks and references to Appendices
HAZEBROUCK H1 CENTRAL	1.7.18	—	Maintenance of Electric Lighting Plant. Work on Brigade in the line Divnl. Batt. Relief of Divisional Line. He went for Light Rgt of Divisional line infantry.	
"	2.7.18		Drawing and repairing funding Elementings. Shooting Brigade. Repairing Camouflage screens	
"	3.7.18		Maintenance of Water Supply of THIEUS, MORBISON Post LINE & LONGWOOD. Main trench & Offrs.	
"	4.7.18		Line 3 water pumps known and continuation of Divisional Camps. Installation of Sheet	
"	5.7.18		Iron Latrine construction & placing Knife Rests in all Posns. Wire ambulances of Observation Post for troops. Artillery 2 M.Gs works M.G. Battn forwarding MG positions	
			Maintenance of Agricultural Plots.	
"	6.7.18 to 15.7.18		Coy Brigade in on 6.7.18 and in construction of Blocks in trenches Preparation of 3 Battn	
			XOYs. Maintenance of Electric Lighting Plant. Survey of 146 Regt sector of Divisional Line	
"	16.7.18 17.7.18		to pt "Cheeror" & Point Helfont Divisional Line; Laying of Railway sleepers. Repairing Camouflage screens.	
"	18.7.18 19.7.18		Drawing & repairing trenches. Repairing & Erecting dugouts. Cleaning & trenching of Ration. Posting & Maintenance	
"	20.7.18		Camouflage screens. Maintenance of Water Supply of MORRISON Post at points formerly of Byss Line and to dugouts thereon. Maintenance of Dugouts before	
			BURMA'S. Maintenance of Agricultural Plots. 2 NCOs with M.G Battn information	
"	21.7.18		MG positions.	
			Inspection by mj. gen. & ay. 6th Division	
	22.7.18 12.30pm		Coy moved by march Route to BARLIN (9.2.b.4.6 FRANCE SHEET 51C).	
BARLIN 9.2.b.4.6	23.7.18		Coy engaged in Intensive training	

Army Form C. 2118.

WAR DIARY
INTELLIGENCE SUMMARY.
(Erase heading not required.)

Instructions regarding War Diaries and Intelligence
Summaries are contained in F. S. Regs., Part II.
and the Staff Manual respectively. Title pages
will be prepared in manuscript.

Place	Date	Hour	Summary of Events and Information	Remarks and references to Appendices
BARLIN	24.4.18		Coy Engaged in Intensive Training.	
92.D.4.6.	25.4.18		" " " " "	
"	26.4.18		" " " " "	
"	27.4.18		" " " " "	
"	28.4.18		" " " " "	
"	29.4.18		" " " " "	
"	30.4.18	9.35 am	Coy moves to ECOIVRES (	
ECOIVRES	31.4.18	4 a.m.	Coy moves to A 26 d 8 y MAROEUIL MAP 1/20000 and looks over R.E. work in Right Sector	
			of Divisional Line ARRAS Sector	

Army Form C. 2118.

WAR DIARY
or
INTELLIGENCE SUMMARY.
(Erase heading not required.)

Instructions regarding War Diaries and Intelligence Summaries are contained in F. S. Regs., Part II. and the Staff Manual respectively. Title pages will be prepared in manuscript.

Place	Date	Hour	Summary of Events and Information	Remarks and references to Appendices
	30.6.18		MONTHLY STRENGTH STATISTICS	

	EFFECTIVE STRENGTH		RATION STRENGTH		DETACHED FOR DUTY		ADMITTED TO FIELD AMB STILL ON STRENGTH	
	OFFS	ORS	OFFS	ORS	OFFS	ORS	OFFS	ORS
CASUALTIES DURING MONTH	0	0	0	0	0	0	0	0
	1	208	5	199	1	26	0	1
STRUCK OFF STRENGTH O. ORS. TO HOSPITAL SICK (TRANSFERRED)	9 1	1 10						
TAKEN ON STRENGTH 0. ORS REINFORCEMENTS FROM BASE	1	10 195						
FROM H'TSP'L		4						
" U.K.	1							
	6	202	5	199	1	30	1	3

| 31.4.18 | | | | |

WAR DIARY
OF
491st (Low Field) Coy R.E.
From 1/8/16 to 31/8/18.

Vol. 4 No 2

War Diary
of
410th (Lowland) Field Coy R.E.
From 31/8/16 to 31/8/18.
Vol A No 2.

WAR DIARY
INTELLIGENCE SUMMARY
(Erase heading not required.)

Army Form C. 2118.

Place	Date	Hour	Summary of Events and Information	Remarks and references to Appendices
ECURIE A.28.c	1/8/18 to 16/8/18		Bn. at Work on Right flank of Divisional Line. Construction of Water Supply and Evacuation of Mined Dugouts. Improving of Trenches. Construction of Minied Dugouts, Construction of Fire Bays, upkeep, repair & maintenance of ROCLINCOURT Rifle Range. Observation, Weapons Training of Rifle Bays.	FRANCE SHEET 51.B
"	16/8/18 2pm		Bn moved to LA MAISON AUBIGNY ROUGE	
LA MAISON ROUGE D.12.c	17/8/18		Bn engaged in intensive training	FRANCE SHEET 51.c
"	18/8/18		" " "	
"	19/8/18		" " "	
"	20/8/18 11.45pm		Bn moved to LATTRE ST QUENTIN	
LATTRE ST QUENTIN J.24.c	21/8/18		Company Resting	
"	22/8/18 11.0pm		Bn moved to BRETENCOURT	— Co —
BRETENCOURT R.24.c.8.9	23/8/18		Bn arrived BRETENCOURT at 2am. Bn moved forward was and forward arriving at Reduced Quinta at 2.55am and taking up Battle Stations at 5.5.a.22 at 4.5am. Zero hour was at 4.55am. Block was built in MARTIN trench at 7.1.b.3.5, HENIN trench, 9 LONG ALLEY Block & Wire obstructions and 500 yards wire entanglements.	
"	24/8/18		Guards Bn moved to BELLACOURT O.31.a. Transfer of 5 Nucleos moved to MERCATEL SWITCH S.3.a.0.5. Forward Divisional moved on 23/8/18	

B.K. Rollins
L.L. Major RE

WAR DIARY
or
INTELLIGENCE SUMMARY.
(Erase heading not required.)

Army Form C. 2118.

Place	Date	Hour	Summary of Events and Information	Remarks and references to Appendices
MERCATEL SWITCH S.3.c.0.5.	25/8/18	3.30pm	Coy H.Q. moved to S.4.c.6.3. Forward Dugout continues as on 23/8/18.	FRANCE SHEET 51b.S.W.
	26/8/18	4.0pm	Coy moved to S.5.b.4.8. Reconnaissance made of Roads leading from MERCATEL to and through BOISLEUX AU MONT, and BOISLEUX ST MARC, and Report on Wells in BOISLEUX AU MONT and BOISLEUX ST MARC. Report on River COJEUL Watersupply. WHILLY WATER supply HENIN, ST MARTIN, HENINEL. Report on Roads to HENIN, ST MARTIN, HENINEL and CHERISY. Report on River SENSEE. Coy engaged on development of Water Supplies, assisting Battalion Commanders in obtaining and improving Coy inclusion Watersupply.	
S.5.b.4.8.	27.8.18		Coy engaged as on 26/8/18. Road across Railway in Branches at BOISLEUX AU MONT. Reconn./varying and Reporting on Forward R.E Dumps	
"	28.8.18		Coy engaged as on 24/8/18. Digging Jack and improvement of MARTIN TRENCH, HENIN TRENCH and SPINNEY AVENUE. Standing order to 42nd Div Coy R.E. and forwarding to 7th Coy in local trench for all Roads and Water Supplies. Coy employed in Road making and preparing new Roads.	
"	29.8.18		Coy engaged as on 29/8/18	
"	30.8.18		" " " 30/8/18.	
"	31.8.18			
"	31.8.18	4.0pm	Coy moved to CROISELLES T.23.a.8.5.	

WAR DIARY
INTELLIGENCE SUMMARY

Army Form C. 2118.

MONTHLY STRENGTH STATISTICS

Place	CASUALTIES	EFFECTIVE STRENGTH		RATION STRENGTH		DETACHED FOR DUTY		ADMITTED TO FIELD AMB		STILL ON STRENGTH		REMARKS
		O	ORs	O	ORs	O	ORs	O	ORs	O	ORs	
31/7/18	DURING MONTH	6	202	5	169			30	1	3		x Includes 4 o/ks admitted to Hospital Crossed N.Y.D.
	STRUCK OFF STRENGTH											
	TO HOSPITAL SICK	-	19									
	TRANSFERRED	1	19*									
		1	19	1	19							
				5	183							
	TAKEN ON											
	REINFORCEMENTS	1	12									
	FROM BASE		6									
	" HOSP.		18	1	18							
31/8/18		6	201	6	162			34	-	5		

5 - 2 Div

CONFIDENTIAL
WAR DIARY
OF
A/2TH (LOWLAND) FIELD Coy RE.

FROM. 1-9-18
TO 30-9-18

VOL 4 N° 3.

Army Form C. 2118.

WAR DIARY
INTELLIGENCE SUMMARY
(Erase heading not required.)

VOL 4. N° 3.

Instructions regarding War Diaries and Intelligence Summaries are contained in F.S. Regs., Part II. and the Staff Manual respectively. Title pages will be prepared in manuscript.

Place	Date	Hour	Summary of Events and Information	Remarks and references to Appendices
CROISILLES T.23.a.8.5	1.9.18		Coy engaged on water outlets at CROISILLES. Reconnaissance of Road to BULLECOURT & of BULLECOURT Water Supply.	SHEET FRANCE 51b SW
"	2.9.18		Maintenance Water Supply CROISILLES. Development of Water Supply BULLECOURT. Reconnaissance of Road to QUEANT.	
"	3.9.18		Water Supply Maintenance Water Supply CROISILLES & BULLECOURT. Reconnaissance QUEANT (D.2 Central) fresh party left in charge Water Supplies CROISILLES & BULLECOURT.	
"		1800	Coy move to QUEANT.	
QUEANT D.2 CENTRAL	4.9.18		Maintenance Water Supplies CROISILLES & BULLECOURT & Development of Water Supplies QUEANT	FRANCE 57c NE
"	5.9.18		Reconnaissance Wells in HIRONDAIRE Bos in South side of NOREUIL - QUEANT Road	
"	6.9.18		Maintenance Water Supplies at CROISILLES, BULLECOURT & QUEANT	
"	7.9.18		Coy engaged Boring on 5.9.18 & Development Water Supplies PRONVILLE Reconnaissance of Wells at NOREUIL.	
"	8.9.18	1000	Maintenance of Water Supplies at CROISILLES, BULLECOURT, QUEANT & PRONVILLE. Squads engaged in renewing Field Coy	
ST LEGER 9.9.18 to 15.9.18 T.24.a.3.6.	9.9.18		Coy moves to ST LEGER (T.24.a.3.6.) Coy engaged on Water Supplies at ST LEGER. Building Hy 63rd Division Maintenance of Rifle Ranges Preparing Notice Boards for 156 Bde. Coy engaged in Musketry training	
"	16.9.18	1330	Coy moves to QUEANT.	
QUEANT D.2 CENTRAL	17.9.18		Coy engaged in Water Supply QUEANT, PRONVILLE & Reconnaissance of Water Supply Wynring	
"	18.9.18		Coy engaged in Water Supply QUEANT & PRONVILLE & Reconnaissance of Water Supply Wynring MOEUVRES. Various Parties engaged at MOEUVRES on RE work in the line. Bn. movements from MOEUVRES & CANAL-du-NORD.	
"	25.9.18		Reconnaissance of Roads surrounding & leading to MOEUVRES & CANAL-du-NORD	
"	26.9.18		Coy engaged on Water outlines QUEANT & PRONVILLE RE work in the line Coy blanketing during Coys. Repairing new Battle Hdq. for Battns in HINDENBURG LINE. Making Saddles, Notice Boards & Goo Blanket frames	

A. S. Mitchell Capt. R.E.
O.C. Hgh Road Field Coy R.E.

Army Form C. 2118.

Instructions regarding War Diaries and Intelligence
Summaries are contained in F. S. Regs., Part II.
and the Staff Manual respectively. Title pages
will be prepared in manuscript.

WAR DIARY
~~INTELLIGENCE~~ SUMMARY.
(Erase heading not required.)

Place	Date	Hour	Summary of Events and Information	Remarks and references to Appendices
QUEANT 2 CENTRAL	24.9.18		Parties consolidating (LEOPOLD) TRENCH. Searching for Booby Traps - booting + Work on Crossing CANAL-DU-NORD) at E.20.a.8.6. Water Supplies at QUEANT + PRONVILLE + Development of water supplies MOEUVRES. Improving Roads approaches and Crossing at CANAL-DU-NORD) and forward.	SHEET FRANCE 57 c. N.E.
"	28.9.18 7.9.18 29.9.18		Watering Horses QUEANT & PRONVILLE + MOEUVRES. Work on Crossing at CANAL-DU-NORD) + Improvement to Road.	
"	30.9.18		Bear HQ moved to MOEUVRES. Coy engaged as on 29.9.18.	

R. Mitchell

WAR DIARY

INTELLIGENCE SUMMARY
(Erase heading not required.)

Army Form C. 2118.

Place	Date	Hour	Summary of Events and Information	Remarks and references to Appendices
X.9.				
	31-8-18		**MONTHLY STRENGTH STATISTICS**	
				EFFECTIVE STRENGTH / RATION STRENGTH / DETACHED FOR DUTY / ADMITTED TO FIELD AMB STILL ON STRENGTH / REMARKS
			CASUALTIES DURING MONTH — O. ORs / O. ORs / O. ORs / O. ORs	
			— / 6 201 / 6 162 / — 34 / 5	
			STRUCK OFF STRENGTH O. ORs	
			TO HOSPITAL SICK — 20	
			TRANSFERRED — —	
			TO HOSPITAL WOUNDED — 2	
			22	
			6 199	
			TAKEN ON O. ORs	
			REINFORCEMENTS 11	
			FROM BASE 9	
			" HOSP 0 20	
	30-9-18		6 199 / 6 163* / — 36 / 3	
			*Includes Hosp. Persons N/B	

R W Murrell

CONFIDENTIAL

WAR DIARY
OF
412TH (LOWLAND) FIELD Coy RE

From 1-9-18
To 30-9-18

VOL. 4. No 3

CONFIDENTIAL

WAR DIARY
OF
A 427TH (LOW) FIELD) COY RE
Vol A No 3.
MONTH OF OCTOBER
1918

CONFIDENTIAL

Vol 7
52 Divn

WAR DIARY OF.
412TH (LOW) (FIELD) COY. RE
Vol. 4 N° 3
MONTH OF OCTOBER

Army Form C. 2118.

WAR DIARY

INTELLIGENCE SUMMARY.

(Erase heading not required.)

Instructions regarding War Diaries and Intelligence Summaries are contained in F. S. Regs., Part II. and the Staff Manual respectively. Title pages will be prepared in manuscript.

Month of OCTOBER 1918

Vol. 4. No. 3

Place	Date	Hour	Summary of Events and Information	Remarks and references to Appendices
MOEUVRES E.20.a.5	1/10/18	0800	Headquarters & two sections moved to GRAINCOURT (K 6 a 2.4) 2 sections moved to CANTAING (F 28 a 2.4) & left over bridges	FRANCE SHEET. 57 N.E. 1/20,000
GRAINCOURT (K 6 a 2.4)	2/10/18	0900 / 1500	Headquarters & two sections moved to CANTAING (F.28.a.2.4) Coy handed over bridges to H3R Field Coy RE & moved to GRAINCOURT (K 6 a 2.4)	FRANCE SHEET 51 C 1/40,000
GRAINCOURT K 6 a 2.4	3/10/18 5/10/18		Development & maintenance of water supply in GRAINCOURT & ANNEUX.	
"	6/10/18	1000	Coy moved to BEAUMETZ LES CAMBRAI (J.17 Central.)	
BEAUMETZ (J.17 CENTRAL)	7/10/18	1030	Coy moved by tactical train & transport by road to VILLERS SIR SIMON (I 5 a.8.8.)	
VILLERS SIR SIMON (I 5 a.8.8.)	8/10/18		Coy resting & cleaning up.	
	9/10/18	0930	Coy moved to DENIER (I 19 c.6.9)	
DENIER I 19.c.6.9.	10/10/18 to 13/10/18		Coy engaged in intensive training Coy refitted	
"	14/10/18		General holiday for Divnl. R.E. Sports.	
"	15/10/18 16/10/18 17/10/18		Intensive training & refitting	
"	19/10/18	0900	Coy moved to CHATEAU DE LA HAIE (2.H.9.4)	
CHATEAU DE LA HAIE	20/10/18	0930	Coy moved to BILLY MONTIGNY (O 26 a1.)	SHEET 44 a 1/40,000
BILLY MONTIGNY (O.26.a.)	21/10/18	0900	Coy moved to HYBY (Q 33.a.6.1.) & commenced construction of a heavy trestle bridge to carry 5 ton axle load over CANAL DE LA HAUTE DEULE (Q 32 6 7)	LENS. 1/100,000

A7093 W: W28 9M1293 750,000 1/17. D. D & L. Ltd. Forms/C2118/14.

Army Form C. 2118.

WAR DIARY
INTELLIGENCE SUMMARY

(Erase heading not required.)

Instructions regarding War Diaries and Intelligence Summaries are contained in F.S. Regs., Part II. and the Staff Manual respectively. Title pages will be prepared in manuscript.

Place	Date	Hour	Summary of Events and Information	Remarks and references to Appendices
RUBY (9.33.a.6.1)	22/10/18		Construction of Trestle Bridge	FRANCE. SHEET 44A 1/40,000.
"	23/10/18		Bridge completed & Coy moved to RACHE (R.32.c.2.4.)	
RACHE R.32.c.2.4.	24/10/18		Construction of Heavy Trestle Bridge to carry 5 ton axle load over the R. LE GODION at (R.32.c.6.5.)	FRANCE:- SHEET 44 1/20,000
"	25/10/18 1030		Trestle Bridge completed. Coy moved to ORCHIES (G.23.d.4.6.)	
ORCHIES G.23.d.4.6.	26/10/18		Repairs to Roads, Collection of Bridging Timbers	
"	27/10/18 1000		Coy moved to LE SAUBOIS (O6.c.3.4.)	
LE SAUBOIS	28/10/18 to 31/10/18		Reconnaissance of forward areas & Bridge sites. Construction of Canvas-covered Rafts & Footbridge.	

Army Form C. 2118.

WAR DIARY
or
INTELLIGENCE SUMMARY.

(Erase heading not required.)

Instructions regarding War Diaries and Intelligence Summaries are contained in F. S. Regs., Part II. and the Staff Manual respectively. Title pages will be prepared in manuscript.

Place	Date	Hour	Summary of Events and Information	Remarks and references to Appendices
			MONTHLY STRENGTH STATISTICS	

		EFFECTIVE STRENGTH		RATION STRENGTH		DETACHED FOR DUTY		ADMITTED TO FIELD AMB STILL ON STRENGTH		REMARKS
	CASUALTIES	O.	ORs	O.	ORs	O.	ORs	O.	ORs	
30-9-18	DURING MONTH	6	199	6	163	–	36	–	3	
	STRUCK OFF STRENGTH. O. ORs									
	TO HOSPITAL SICK. – 11									
	TRANSFERED 1-0									
	KILLED IN ACTION 1-0									
	TO HOSPITAL WOUNDED – 2 11									
		4	188							
	TAKEN ON O. ORs									
	REINFORCEMENTS 2 13									
	FROM BASE									
	HOSP. 3 2 16									
31-10-18		6	204	4	163	2	41	–	–	

A7092   W: W 125 9/M 1793 750,000. 1/17. D. D & L. Ltd Forms/C 2118/4.

CONFIDENTIAL

Vol 8

WAR DIARY.
OF
4/107th (LOWLAND) FIELD Coy. R.E.

Vol. No. 4
No. 4

WAR DIARY
INTELLIGENCE SUMMARY
(Erase heading not required.)

Army Form C. 2118.

MONTH OF NOVEMBER 1918
VOL 7 N° 7

Place	Date	Hour	Summary of Events and Information	Remarks and references to Appendices
LE SAUBOIS 06 C.3.Y.	1/11/18		Reconnaissance of ToeSail Areas & Bridging sites. Construction of Canvas Covered Rafts & Trestleges.	FRANCE SHEET 77
"	2/11/18 to 4/11/18		Coy engaged in fabrication of "JERUSALEM" rafts (canvas covered) and Trestleges.	1/20,000
"	5/11/18		On crossing RIVER ESCAUT & JARD CANAL and cutting material for heavy bridges.	"
"			One section assisting 156 Inf. Brigade on the line, strengthening cellars, and putting up camouflage.	"
"	8/11/18		Company (less Leath) Bridges across RIVER ESCAUT & JARD CANAL and providing Ferries for inundation between LEES artesians. 156 Brigade and Corps Cyclists	"
"	9/11/18		Both forces across inundation. Preparation of Trestles for Heavy Bridges across RIVER ESCAUT & JARD CANAL.	"
"	9/11/18		Company engaged on Heavy Bridging across RIVER ESCAUT & JARD CANAL at HERGNIES. (VALENCIENNES SHEET 12. G.1.3.4). Coy moved to HERGNIES on 9-11-18 at 16.00. Bridge handed over to 12th Scott. RE	"
HERGNIES G.1.3.Y	12/11/18	0930	Company marched to SIRAULT. (TOURNAI SHEET 5. J.6.4.2.	VALENCIENNES SHEET 12
SIRAULT J.6.4.2	13/11/18		Company engaged on overhauling & blocking equipment.	TOURNAI SHEETS
"	14/11/18 to 18/11/18		Company engaged on Training, Kit Inspections. Overhauling & blocking Pontoon & Trestle Equipment.	
"	19/11/18	1000	Company moved to GHLIN (VALENCIENNES SHEET 12. K.1. 85.45.) @	

N. Willoughby RE
OC 111??

Army Form C. 2118.

WAR DIARY
or
INTELLIGENCE SUMMARY.
(Erase heading not required.)

Instructions regarding War Diaries and Intelligence Summaries are contained in F. S. Regs., Part II. and the Staff Manual respectively. Title pages will be prepared in manuscript.

Place	Date	Hour	Summary of Events and Information	Remarks and references to Appendices
GHLIN. X.1. 55. 45.	20/11/18		Coy engaged Sawing, Cleaning Wagons Junior making Targets for Rifle Range	VALENCIENNES SHEET 12.
	21/11/18		Company engaged as on 20/11/18.	
	22/11/18		Company Limbers in full marching order paraded for inspection at 6 R.E.	"
	23/11/18		Company engaged in Sawing. Cleaning Limbers Equipment. Making & Opening Targets. Making & Painting Notice Boards. Making Rifle Range.	"
	25/11/18		Company moved to MASNY ST PIERRE @ 1300 on 25/11/18.	
MASNY ST PIERRE E.14. b 3. y.	26/11/18 to 30/11/18		Company engaged in cleaning Wagons Limbers Equipment. Inspection making & Painting Notice Boards. Making Rifle Range. Opening Targets.	TOURNAI SHEET 5.

N Wellesley Pain? Ct.
O.C. 111th Field Co.

WAR DIARY
or
INTELLIGENCE SUMMARY.
(Erase heading not required.)

Army Form C. 2118.

Instructions regarding War Diaries and Intelligence Summaries are contained in F. S. Regs., Part II. and the Staff Manual respectively. Title pages will be prepared in manuscript.

Place	Date	Hour	Summary of Events and Information	Remarks and references to Appendices
	31·10·18		MONTHLY STRENGTH STATISTICS CASUALTIES DURING MONTH — EFFECTIVE STRENGTH: O. 0, 6 204 / RATION STRENGTH: O. 4 163 / DETACHED FOR DUTY: 0 2 41 / ADMITTED TO FIELD AMB STILL ON STRENGTH: 0 0 0 / REMARKS STRUCK OFF STRENGTH:- TO HOSPITAL SICK — O. O/R 5 / 6 199 TAKEN ON STRENGTH REINFORCEMENTS FROM BASE — O. O/R 1 12 / 1 12	
	30·11·18		4 211 5 190 2 19 0 0 2	6 Wellington Regt

WAR DIARY

OF

AUSTRALIAN 2ND (FIELD) COYRE

FROM 1/11/18
TO 30/11/18

MONTH OF NOVEMBER 1918

VOL. 4
No. 4

- Confidential -

War Diary
of
412th (Lowland) Field Coy. R.E.
from 1st December 1918
to 31st December 1918.

(Volume 4. No 6.)

WAR DIARY

INTELLIGENCE SUMMARY

Army Form C. 2118.

MONTH OF DECEMBER 1918
VOL. 4. No 6.

(Erase heading not required.)

Instructions regarding War Diaries and Intelligence Summaries are contained in F. S. Regs, Part II. and the Staff Manual respectively. Title pages will be prepared in manuscript.

Place	Date	Hour	Summary of Events and Information	Remarks and references to Appendices
MASNUY ST. PIERRE. E.14.b.3.7.	1/12/18 to 7/12/18		Company engaged on training, cleaning wagons, equipment &c. Making & painting Notice Boards. Making Rifle range & sharpening targets. Making Incinerator & Latrine seats. Improvement of Billets. Collecting stalks & placing in dumps.	TOURNAI SHEET 5. 1/100,000
	8/12/18		Major H.J. Davies assumed command of Company. M.C.R.E.(T) Company engaged as on 7/12/18.	
	9/12/18 to 12/12/18		Company engaged as on 8/12/18.	
	13/12/18		Company marched to LOUVIGNIES. (BELGIUM SHEET 38. W.10.b.8.8.) renamed at MASNUY ST. PIERRE.	
LOUVIGNIES. W.10.b.8.8.	14/12/18 to 16/12/18		Company engaged on training, cleaning wagons &c. Making & painting notice boards. Making Latrine seats. Improvement of Billets. Making rifle range & sharpening targets. Company transport engaged in removing R.E. materials from old to new workshop.	BELGIUM SHEET 38. 1:40,000
	17/12/18		Company transport paraded in full marching order for inspection by Divisional Commander.	
	18/12/18		Company engaged as on 16/12/18. Range party reported Company.	
	19/12/18 to 23/12/18		Company engaged on cleaning wagons. Making & painting notice boards, making Latrine seats, Incinerator & Cookhouse, & improvement of Models for huts in Brigade area.	
	24/12/18		Company engaged as on 23/12/18. Capt. G.A. Beattie R.E. assumed command of Company.	
	25/12/18		Company engaged in Sports.	

Army Form C. 2118.

WAR DIARY
INTELLIGENCE SUMMARY.
(Erase heading not required.)

Place	Date	Hour	Summary of Events and Information	Remarks and references to Appendices
LOUVIGNIES W.16.6.88.	26/12/18 to 31/12/18		Company engaged in making latrine seats, incinerators, cookhouses & improvement of billets for units in Brigade area.	BELGIUM SHEET 38.

J. Meates Capt RE
O.C. 412 Field Coy RE.

Army Form C. 2118.

WAR DIARY
INTELLIGENCE SUMMARY
(Erase heading not required.)

Place	Date	Hour	Summary of Events and Information	Remarks and references to Appendices
			MONTHLY STRENGTH STATISTICS:	

CASUALTIES	EFFECTIVE STRENGTH		RATION STRENGTH		DETACHED FOR DUTY		ADMITTED TO FIELD AMB. STILL ON STRENGTH		REMARKS
DURING MONTH.	O.	OR's.	O.	OR's.	O.	OR's.	O.	OR's.	
30-11-16	7	-211	5	-190	2	19.			
STRUCK OFF STRENGTH:- 0 OR's 13 TO HOSPITAL SICK		13 / 7-198							
TAKEN ON STRENGTH 0. OR's REINFORCEMENTS FROM BASE	-	6	-	6					
31/12/16	7	204	7	184	-	20			GMB

Confidential

War Diary
of
412th (Lowland) Field Co. R.E.
from 1st December 1918
to 31st December 1918

(Volume 4. No 6)

CONFIDENTIAL

WAR DIARY.
412 (Lowland) Field Coy. R.E.
Month of January 1919
Vol. 4.   No. 8.

Army Form C. 2118.

WAR DIARY
or
INTELLIGENCE SUMMARY.
(Erase heading not required.)

MONTH OF JANUARY 1919
VOL 4 No 8

Instructions regarding War Diaries and Intelligence Summaries are contained in F.S. Regs., Part II. and the Staff Manual respectively. Title pages will be prepared in manuscript.

Place	Date	Hour	Summary of Events and Information	Remarks and references to Appendices
LOUVIGNIES WD D 83. SHEET 38 1:40,000 EDITION 2A BELGIUM	1/1/19		Company engaged in Sports.	
	2/1/19		Making Table for Dining Hall. New Cookhouse. painting & cleaning wagons making Truncheons & Candle Sticks, working on roads.	
	3/1/19			
	4/1/19		repairing of Pontoon wagons & painting same	
	5/1/19			
	6/1/19		Company engaged in repairs of Dining hall & Cookhouse, varnishing Pontoon equipment.	
	7/1/19			
	8/1/19		Inspection of Company. An Divisional ceremonial Parade by 22nd Corps General.	
	9/1/19 to		Company engaged in repairs of Dining hall & Cookhouse, varnishing pontoon equipment. Tinsmith making tin buckets. Painters Painting all Stable Huts. Painting walls etc, Plumbers working or Clapper quarry. Repairing of harness. Bridging material varnished. Repairing of Dining Room floor.	
	16/1/19			
	17/1/19 to 18/1/19		Company engaged repairing of Dining Room erecting Notice Boards, Painting Numbers.	
	19/1/19		C in C of Company on visit to Waterloo remainder on sports	
	20/1/19		Company engaged in Sports.	
	21/1/19		Company engaged in repairs of Cookhouses, making of hurdles, road scrapers Tin pots Knife battle. Painting of Tool carts. Inspection of Tool Carts.	
	25/1/19			
	26/1/19			
	27/1/19		Visiting Waterloo, making Latrines & Aldershot Ovens. Painting Div sign on wagons, repairing doors of Dunnage.	
	31/1/19			

G.M. Heather
Captain R.E.
O.C. 412" L.S.W. Fd. Coy. T.F.

WAR DIARY
or
INTELLIGENCE SUMMARY.

Army Form C. 2118.

Place	Date	Hour	Summary of Events and Information	Remarks and references to Appendices

MONTHLY STRENGTH STATISTICS

	EFFECTIVE STRENGTH		RATION STRENGTH		DETACHED FOR DUTY		ADMITTED FIELD AMB STILL ON STRENGTH		REMARKS
CASUALTIES	O.	OR	O.	OR	O.	OR	O.	OR	
	4	204	4.	184	-	20.	-	-	
31/12/18 STRUCK OFF STRENGTH O. ORS TO HOSPITAL SICK	-	-							
TAKEN ON STRENGTH O.ORS -2 REINFORCEMENTS FROM BASE 31-1-19.	8.	206	4 -	153	2.	13		3	

CONFIDENTIAL

WAR DIARY
OF
412TH (LOWLAND) FIELD COMPANY, ROYAL ENGINEERS.

1ST FEBRUARY   TO   28TH FEBRUARY   1919.

H. Helliwell LIEUT. R.E.
O/C 412TH
Low. Fd. Coy. R.E.

Army Form C. 2118.

WAR DIARY
or
INTELLIGENCE SUMMARY.
(Erase heading not required.)

Instructions regarding War Diaries and Intelligence Summaries are contained in F. S. Regs., Part II. and the Staff Manual respectively. Title pages will be prepared in manuscript.

Place	Date	Hour	Summary of Events and Information	Remarks and references to Appendices
Sauvigny	1st Sept.	0900	Inspection, engaged in repairs, village improvements & general cleaning up of Units Area.	
"	2nd "	"	" " & Church Parade.	
"	3rd,4th,5th "	"	General clean up, village improvements, Latrines, Aldershot Ovens, Box for Sports gear, Inventory Boards, sign Boards + cleaning harness.	
"	6,7,8 "	"	Inspection. Sign Boards erected at Sauvigny, village improvements, Box for Sports gear, Latrines, Mess cafe, Butter case, Repairing stables, removing & fitting benches.	
"	9th "	"	Church Parade.	
"	10,11,12 "	"	" "	
"	13th "	"	Minor repairs to billets, door of Chateau, door of Cookhouse, Dining Hall, Latrines, remainder bagging Harness.	
"	14th "	"	Petit Theatre repairs, erecting & fitting stage with scenery etc.	
"	15th "	"	Minor repairs + B.H.Q.	
"	16th "	"	Repairing Dining Hall floor, various repairs & general clean up around village.	
"	17,18,19,20 "	"	Church Parade.	
"	21st,22nd "	"	Various repairs & improvements, finish erect cookhouse at B.H.Q. & junior repairs floor of dining Hall.	
"	"	"	Loaded up & sent two Wilden trestles, two bags superstructure complete for XXII Corps Race Course, minor repairs to billets.	
"	23rd "	"	Inspection & Church Parade.	
"	"	"	" "	
"	24th "	"	Repair overhead rail for sliding door at Chateau stables, various minor village improvements.	
"	25,26 "	"	XXII Corps Race Course, Party sent for duty.	
"	27 "	"	" Races. Party sent for duty.	
"	28 "	"	General clean up on Coy. Area + various minor improvements.	

Army Form C. 2118.

WAR DIARY
or
INTELLIGENCE SUMMARY.
(Erase heading not required.)

Instructions regarding War Diaries and Intelligence Summaries are contained in F. S. Regs., Part II. and the Staff Manual respectively. Title pages will be prepared in manuscript.

Place	Date	Hour	Summary of Events and Information	Remarks and references to Appendices

MONTHLY STRENGTH STATISTICS.

		EFFECTIVE STRENGTH		RATION STRENGTH		DETACHED FOR DUTY.		ADMITTED TO FIELD AMBULANCE STILL ON STRENGTH.		Remarks
		O	ORs	O	ORs	O	ORs	O	ORs	
CASUALTIES	31-1-19	8	206	4	153	2	13		3	
Struck off Strength 0 ORs										
To Hospital Sick - 1										
Taken on Strength 0 ORs										
Reinforcements from Base + 1	28-2-19	8	207	3	69	1	2		1	

Strength Statistic (Actual)

Officers	Other Ranks	Animals			Reasons For Changes In Strength
		Riders	L.D'	Mules.	
4	75	6	14	15	2 Officers + 127 other ranks have proceeded on Demobilization 2 Other Ranks are on leave 2 Other Ranks are in Hospital. The reduction in the Animal Strength has been caused through (1) the Demobilizing of Animals (2) the Return to Veterinary Section.

N. Wellwell
Lieut.
~~Captain~~ R.E.
o/c 412th Low. Fd. Coy. R.E.

412TH
(LOWLAND) FIELD
COMPANY, R.E.

Date: 1-3-19

WAR DIARY

FOR

MONTH MARCH 1919.

Vol 12

Army Form C. 2118.

WAR DIARY
or
INTELLIGENCE SUMMARY.
(Erase heading not required.)

Instructions regarding War Diaries and Intelligence
Summaries are contained in F. S. Regs., Part II.
and the Staff Manual respectively. Title pages
will be prepared in manuscript.

Place	Date	Hour	Summary of Events and Information	Remarks and references to Appendices
Louvignies Hainault Belgium	March 1st	0900	Company engaged on various village repairs. Afternoon devoted to Sports	
"	2nd	"	Rifle Inspection. Church Parade to Chausse Notre Dame.	
"	4th,5th & 6th	"	Daily Inspections. Repair Stables, Doors etc at Chateau. General clean up of round village	
"	7th & 8th	"	General village improvements. Afternoon devoted to sport.	
"	9th, 10th	"	Bury mine at Soignies Station. General Repairs to village	
"	11th	"		
"	12th,13th	"	Cleaning & Repainting Wagons. Returning to R.E. dump. Material in Company Stores	
"	14 & 15	"	General village improvements. Afternoon devoted to Sports Football, etc.	
"	16	"	Church Parade. Court & Danet	
"	17 & 18	"	Repairs. Concert Hall Filter. General Repairs	
"	19,20,21	"	Preparing to move to Soignies. Cleaning up village & leaving it in a clean condition. Received certificate from Bourgemacker as to same.	
"	22	"	Preparing for move to Soignies	
"	23	"	Move To Soignies	
Soignies Hainault Belgium	24, 25 & 26	"	Cleaning up billeting Area. Men making themselves comfortable.	
"	27, 28 & 29	"	Cleaning up Area. Checking stores + various odd jobs	
"	30, 31	"	Erecting Latrine Screens + building ramps at Soignies	

Monthly Strength Statistics

CASUALTIES During Month.	EFFECTIVE STRENGTH		RATION STRENGTH			DETACHED FOR DUTY		ADMITTED TO FIELD AMBULANCE STILL ON STRENGTH		REMARKS
	O	ORS	O	ORS		O	ORS	O	ORS	
	8	207	3	–	69		2		1	
28-2-19 Struck off Strength	0	ORS								
To Hospital Sick –		2								
Transferred	1	9								
Taken on Strength Reinforcements from Base										
31-3-19. " Hospital	1	7	178	2	49	1			2	

412TH
(LOWLAND) FIELD
COMPANY, R.E.

No. _____
Date 31..3..19.

[signature]
Captain R.E.
O.C. 412 (Low. Fd. Coy. T.F.

No 13

WAR DIARY

412TH LOWLAND FIELD Co ROYAL ENGINEERS.

[signature]
Captain R.E.
OC 412th Low. Fd. Coy. T.F.

412TH
(LOWLAND) FIELD
COMPANY, R.E.
No.
Date 1 - 5 - 19

WAR DIARY
or
INTELLIGENCE SUMMARY.
(Erase heading not required.)

Army Form C. 2118.

Instructions regarding War Diaries and Intelligence Summaries are contained in F. S. Regs., Part II. and the Staff Manual respectively. Title pages will be prepared in manuscript.

Place	Date	Hour	Summary of Events and Information	Remarks and references to Appendices
Sequier	APRIL			
Havnault	1st 2nd 3rd	0900	Inspections, erecting latrine screens at station. Greasing saddlery. Marking & stencilling boxes ready for the move home. Cleaning Billets	
Belgium	4th 5th	"	" Repairing Latrine at Station. Cleaning Lewis Guns. General Clean up. Afternoon devoted to Sport	
	6th	"	" Rifle Skeleton Order. Church Parade	
	7th 8th 9th	"	" Cleaning Wagons. General clean-up of Billeting Area. Football Match with No. 1 Section D.A.C.	
	9th 10th 11th	"	" Latrine Screens at Station. Cleaning Wagons. Marking Harness bags & various repairs to billets.	
	12th	"	" Cleaning Lewis Guns. Checking stores on foot carts.	
	13	"	" Rifle Inspection. Cricket Match with 410th Fd. Coy R.E.	
	14th 15th 16th	"	" Inspections. Bathing Parade. Cleaning Billets. Cleaning Lewis Guns. Football Match 4th R.S.	
	17th 18th 19th	"	" Repainting Shafts of Wagon & Divisional Signs. Return all 2 H.A. & D.H.S. Painting hubs & signs on Wagons completed	
	20th	"	" Rifle. Church Parade	
	21st	"	" Holiday	
	22nd 23rd 24th	"	" Inspection. Water Cart taken to Wagon Park to be Painted. Football Match with 1st Batt. R.F.A. on Div Cup. Cleaning Lewis Guns	
	25th 26th	"	" Rifle Inspection. Bathing Parade. all available men Cleaning Wagons Polishing all Brass work on Pontoon Wagons.	
	27	"	Church Parade with 410 & 413th Fld. Coy R.E.	
	28 & 29	"	" Inspections. Cleaning Wagons working at the Station assisting Troops of Division to entrain,	
			" Cleaning Wagons. Making Packing Cases for S.D.0.	

Monthly Strength Statistic.

Casualties During Month	Effective Strength	Ration Strength	Detached For Duty		Admitted to Field Ambulance Still on Strength	Remarks
	0 ORs	0 ORs	0	ORs	0 ORs	
31-3-19	7-178	2-49	2	1	0	
Struck off Strength ORs						
To Hospital Sick 1						
Taken on Strength						
From Base						
From Hospital	7-131	2-50				
30/4/19						

412TH
(LOWLAND) FIELD
COMPANY, R.E.

No. ....
Date. 1/5/19

[signature]
Captain R.E.
O C 412th Low. Fd. Coy. T.F.

CONFIDENTIAL

War Diary.
412 Fd Co RE
Month of
April 1919

Vol. 5
No 4.

Vol 14

Diary of

412th Lowland Field Coy

Royal Engineers

Army Form C. 2118.

WAR DIARY
or
INTELLIGENCE SUMMARY.
(Erase heading not required.)

Instructions regarding War Diaries and Intelligence Summaries are contained in F. S. Regs., Part II. and the Staff Manual respectively. Title pages will be prepared in manuscript.

Place	Date	Hour	Summary of Events and Information	Remarks and references to Appendices
Soignies Belgium	May 1st & 2nd	0900	Inspection. Making Packing cases for storing Saddlery &c. Cleaning Wagons	
	3rd	0900	Inspection. Rifle. Packing cases, fatigue. Bathing Parade to Divisional Baths	
	4	1000	Divine Service	
	5,6,7	0900	Inspection. Cleaning Lewis Guns. Painting G.S. Wagons. Packing Cases. Painting G.S. Wagon Cricket Match 410th v 412th.	
	8,9,10	0900	Cleaning Steelwork of Wagons. Repainting Divisional Signs Cricket Match 412th versus 413th Field Coy	
	11	1000	Divine Service	
	12,13,14	0900	Inspection. Painting Rib Bars of Wagons. Cleaning Brass tops on Jacks to Wagons Making Boxes H12 Field coy RE foiles	
	15,16,17	0900	Inspection. Cleaning Lewis Guns. General Fatigue. Cleaning up Company Area.	
	18th	1000	Divine Service Pay Parade.	
	19-20th	0900	Rifle Inspections. Cleaning up. Afternoon devoted to sport. Cricket Match Divisional Engineers v R.A.M.C.	
	21st	0900	Inspection. Fatigue Party for clearing stone from Ordnance Polishing + Washing all Brasswork on Wagons	
	22nd 23rd	0900	Repainting Divisional Signs General Fatigue + Bathing Parade.	
	24th	0900	Working on Divisional Area Boards Pay Parade.	
	25th	1000	Divine Service	
	26th 27th 28th 29th	0900	Inspection Working on Divisional Area Boards Parties Working on Wagon Park	
	30th 31st	0900	Inspections Working on Divisional Area Boards Cricket Match Divisional R.E's versus 155 Brigade	

Monthly Strength Statistic

Casualties during the Month.		Effective Strength. O OR² OR³	Ration Strength O OR² OR³	Detached for duty. O OR² OR⁵	Admitted to Field Ambulance. Still on Strength. O ORS	Remarks
30/4/19	Struck off Strength OR² To Hospital Sick	7 - 131	2 50	0 1	0 ORS	
31/5/19	Taken on Strength From Base From Hospital	8 79 -	29	1	1	

412TH (LOWLAND) FIELD COMPANY R.E.
No............
Date. 1/6/19

B Stewart
O.C. 412ᵗʰ

Lieut
Captain R.E.
Low. Fd. Coy, T.F.

www.ingramcontent.com/pod-product-compliance
Lightning Source LLC
Chambersburg PA
CBHW081449160426
43193CB00013B/2423